15

I, even I, am He who comforts you. Who are you that you
should be afraid of a man who will die, and of the son of a
man who will be made like grass?
Isaiah 51:12

Lord - Give me the boldness to ask for what I want.
I know that the answer will always be no if I do not make my requests known. I thank you for allowing me to walk freely in your favor, and I bind up the tactics of the enemy that seek to attack my voice.

I speak unprecedented confidence over my life. You validated my worth by calling me yours. Because of this validation, I can be brave in my request to you and the people you've placed on this earth to bless me.

I will not shy away from advocating for the things I want anymore, but instead, I will recall who lives inside of me. By your Spirit, I will ask and receive every blessing you intend for me.

Amen

16

Study to shew thyself approved unto God, a workman that needeth not to be ashamed, rightly dividing the word of truth.
2 Timothy 2:15

*D*ear God - Help me always to maintain a student mentality.

May I never get so cocky that I forget to study to show myself approved. I understand that being the best at what I do requires me to study my craft. I want to be diligent in my pursuit of knowledge so that I can acquire the wisdom to make the right decisions.

I thank you that you will prepare me for promotion, increase, and favor through my commitment to learning. I trust that if I do my part to be ready for your blessing in my career and business endeavors, that you will bless me with the desires of my heart.

Amen

17

Iron sharpens iron, and one man sharpens another.
Proverbs 27:17 ESV

Awesome God - I thank you today for creating divine connections in my life.

Bless me with godly mentors who not only inspire me to achieve my career pursuits but also inspire me to live a life that is pleasing to you. I know that where two or three gather together, you are in the midst. I praise you that you see the areas in my life where I could use an extra nudge and that you have already assigned special people to help me be better in those areas.

I am open to receiving from good counsel, Lord. Orchestrate the right encounters so that I form relationships with experienced leaders who can help me develop my spiritual growth as well as my career growth.

Amen

18

Blessed are those who hunger and thirst for righteousness,
for they shall be satisfied.
Matthew 5:6 ESV

Lord - All the things I hope to accomplish mean nothing without a strong relationship with you.

Keep me steadfast in my endeavors to know you in a better way. I want to seek your face like never before. I am thirsty for an increase in knowledge about your word and hungry for more of you in my day to day experiences. Forgive me for each time I've let life supersede spending quality time with you.

It is because of you that I live and move and have my being. I worship you for who you are, and I praise you for keeping me when I do not deserve to be kept. I am full of dreams and aspirations, but You are my greatest desire. I love you more than anything, and I will forever make you #1 in my life.

Amen

19

Thus also faith by itself, if it does not have works, is dead.
James 2:17 NKJV

God - your word tells us that faith without works is dead. Help me to be the type of woman who works diligently for the things that I want. Do not let me get weary in doing the work. Instead, keep me disciplined by reminding me of my purpose.

I bind the spirit of laziness, and I commit to the labor.

I thank you that you see me in my season of sowing and that you are faithful in your ability to let me reap the harvest of my work. I am dedicated to going the extra mile. I'm sorry for the times that I expected you to give me what I had not made an effort to get. Thank you for the capacity to do. I will not squander this capacity by settling for the spirit of laziness.

Amen

20

*Having gifts that differ according to the grace given to us,
let us use them: if prophecy, in proportion to our faith;
Romans 12:6 ESV*

Jesus - I thank you for every talent that you saw fit to bless me with. Forgive me for not fully utilizing these talents in a way that is pleasing to you.

I want to be busy with the work of using my gifts to be a blessing to the Kingdom of God. Fill me with your heart for humanity. Show me how to use every gifting in a way that helps my fellow man.

I make it my duty to turn my talents into a form of ministry, understanding that no talent is too small to make a difference. I praise you for visions and fresh ideas that tie my talents to your work. I am open and available to you, Lord.

Amen

21

*Walk in wisdom toward outsiders, making the best use of
the time.*
Colossians 4:5 ESV

racious God - Compel me to do the things that I know
I should do. Remove the spirit of procrastination and
give me the will power to complete tasks even when I do
not feel motivated.

Fill me with the surge of energy I need to do the hard
things. I know that belaboring leads to overwhelming
feelings. I want to be at peace so that I can be effective and
efficient. Help me to use my time wisely.

Show me how to plan my day. Be with me as I knock out
the hard stuff that I am tempted to put on the backburner.

Amen

22

*Give thanks in all circumstances; for this is the will of God
in Christ Jesus for you*
1 Thessalonians 5:18 ESV

Lord - I thank you for giving me dreams for my life. As I work to accomplish these dreams, help me to be thankful for where I am right now.

I understand that success is a journey rather than a destination, and I want to enjoy the ride. I know that wishing my life away is a form of anxiety. You have called me to be anxious for nothing. Provide me with the ability to work hard for my future while also being grateful for my present place in life. When the wheels in my head start turning too fast with thoughts of tomorrow, help me recall that you hold the key to all things.

Calm my spirit as only you can.

Amen

23

*The point is this: whoever sows sparingly will also reap
sparingly, and whoever sows bountifully will also reap
bountifully. Each one must give as he has decided in his
heart, not reluctantly or under compulsion, for God loves a
cheerful giver. And God is able to make all grace abound to
you, so that having all sufficiency in all things at all times,
you may abound in every good work.*
2 Corinthians 9:6-8 ESV

Dear Jesus - Give me a heart for community.

I know that each of us is called to a place for a reason. Help me to use my abilities to impact the area around me; use me as a positive community leader. Provide me with the influence to make a difference for you.

Prick my heart with a desire to be involved in community service. Show me which organizations I should invest my time in, and guide me as I research the prevalent needs around me. Make my calling centered on helping those around me. I want to make my city and state a better place.

Shine through me as I do work for you in my community.

Amen

24

The blessing of the Lord makes rich,
and he adds no sorrow with it.
Proverbs 10:22

God - I thank you for increase. I praise you for unexpected blessings in my life. I thank you for raises and residual income. I believe you for more.

Let my businesses, side hustles, and ventures be profitable. Provide me with overflow. Show me how to market myself in a way that gets me before the right audiences and results in more cash flow.

I believe that you have called me to be prosperous. Pour out your blessings in a manner that I do not have room enough to receive all that is in store for me. Use my financial overflow to bless others. I want to be a testimony of your faithfulness even as it relates to my finances.

Amen

25

For am I now seeking the approval of man, or of God? Or am I trying to please man? If I were still trying to please man, I would not be a servant of Christ.
Galatians 1:10 ESV

Protector of my Heart - Remove desires of co-dependency and people-pleasing. Help me to be okay with being disliked.

Put more of my focus on pleasing the Kingdom of God and less of it on satisfying those in the earthly realm. I

know that the anxiety I feel when I try to make everyone happy is counterproductive to my peace. Remind me that it is not my job to worry about the perceptions of others. Let me maintain my joy even when others aren't happy with the decisions I make regarding my life. Take away the pressure of attempting to achieve the impossible by being everything to everybody.

Amen

26

For God so loved the world, that he gave his only begotten
Son, that whosoever believeth in him should not perish,
but have everlasting life.
John 3:16 KJV

Ruler of my Soul - You showed the ultimate sacrifice by giving your son for our sins. May I be selfless like you by giving more than I can take.

I do not want my own desires to cloud my ability to give to others. Compel me to use my time, efforts, and resources to help others.

Use me as a mentor to those coming behind me and a blessing to those in need. I want to be the type of friend and family member who helps those I love by adding value to my relationships rather than always expecting to receive. Use me as a vessel through which blessings flow.

Amen

27

Do not seek what you should eat or what you should drink, nor have an anxious mind.
Luke 12: 29

Jehovah Jirah - Take away feelings of anxiety that disturb my peace of mind.

When I consider my needs and desires, I am sometimes overwhelmed with thoughts that leave me worried and anxious. During these times, I need the calmness of the Holy Spirit to remind me that all things work together for the good of those who love you. Don't let me carry the burden of things I cannot control. Instead, be the present help that I need.

Soothe my mind by bringing my focus back to you and your greatness. I know that you consider my best interest and that you will provide exactly what I need when I need it most. Thank you, Father.

Amen

28

Be strong and of good courage, do not fear nor be afraid of them; for the Lord your God, He is the One who goes with you. He will not leave you or forsake you.
Deuteronomy 31:6

*D*ear Lord - Right now I cast out fear. With you on my side, I know there is nothing that I should be afraid of.

Help me to be strong and of good courage when I am tempted to be fearful. Your word says that you will never leave me or forsake me. Because of this fact, I can confidently rely on your might in every situation that makes me nervous. I know that you have the final say. I trust you to guide and protect me from all of my worst nightmares.

I rest in your protection.

Amen

29

*He delivers me from my enemies. You also lift me above
those who rise against me; You have delivered me from the
violent man.*
Psalms 18:48

Father - Change my outlook on enemies and opposition.
Teach me how to handle disagreements with wisdom
and grace.

I trust you to handle situations that I cannot. I believe
in your power to rectify misunderstandings and to move
anything that seeks to hinder me in any way. I thank you
for turning around negative encounters and working them
out for my good. Even through the discomfort I feel, let my
attitude serve as a witness for you.

Lift me above those who rise against me. Help me lead
others to Christ by how I respond to my enemies.

Amen

30

Cast your burden on the Lord, and He shall sustain you;
He shall never permit the righteous to be moved.
Psalm 55:22 NIV

She came and worshipped Him, saying, "Lord, help me!"
Matthew 15:25

God - I cry out to you today for your help.

Sometimes the stress of life leaves me feeling overwhelmed, tired, and confused. I want to trade these feelings for your peace. Right now I cast my burdens on you. I trust you to sustain me when I cannot sustain myself, and I thank you in advance that you will never allow me to be moved by stressful moments in my life.

Let your spirit comfort me. Give me rest in you, oh Lord.

Amen

31

*You will keep him in perfect peace, whose mind is stayed on
You, because he trusts in You.*
Isaiah 26:3

Heavenly Savior - When life is not going as planned, I
thank you for keeping my mind stayed on you.

I trust you with every personal and professional outcome
in my life. I know that you have the final say regarding all
things. Because of this, I will meditate on your greatness;
understanding that thoughts of You are the key to perfect
peace. I will keep your word present in my mind when
worry, stress, and frustration seek to rob me of the peace
that you paid the ultimate price to grant me.

Amen

32

*Come to Me, all you who labor and are heavy laden, and
I will give you rest. Take my yoke upon you and learn from
Me, for I am gentle and lowly in heart, and you will find
rest for your souls. For My yoke is easy and
My burden is light.*
Matthew 11:28-30

Lord - I thank you that I can come to you when I am feeling tired. Your word says in these moments that you will give me rest for my soul. Right now, I give my burdens over to you, taking comfort in your ability. Because of who you are, I can relax regardless of the circumstances. My worldly problems are no match for your heavenly power.

When the labor of life seems too much, help me to learn from You. I praise you for renewed strength to handle everything that comes my way with energy, grit, and grace.

Amen

33

*For in him we live, and move, and have our being; as
certain also of your own poets have said, For we are also
his offspring.*
Acts 17:28

God - Today, I come asking for nothing but thanking
you for everything.

So often, I am consumed with my wants and desires
that I forget to take time to simply praise you. I realize
that every breath I take is because of your splendor. No
matter my goals and ambitions, I never want to take life
for granted. Right now, I thank you for allowing me to live
and move and have my being. I worship you for calling me
your daughter and allowing me to be your offspring. Thank
you, Lord, for making me in your image and for calling me
yours.

Regardless of what happens today, I will smile because
You are within me.

Amen

34

*Do not despise these small beginnings, for the Lord rejoices
to see the work begin, to see the plumb line in
Zerubbabel's hand.*
Zechariah 4:10 NLT

Father - Help me not to despise small beginnings.

Sometimes, I am so focused on where I want to be that I turn my nose up at where I am right now in my life. However, your word says that You rejoice to see the work begin. I am blessed to know that it is the work I put in now that is pleasing unto you. As I diligently labor, You are laying the framework for bigger and better. I realize that to reap more, I must first start.

Thank you for reminding me that small beginnings are valuable to you.

Amen

35

*And let us not grow weary of doing good, for in due season
we will reap, if we do not give up.*
Galatians 6:9 ESV

Lord - I admit that I get frustrated when I am doing the right thing but do not seem to be making the progress that I would like to see. Help me not to grow weary in well-doing. I know that I have to keep going to reap the harvest that you have stored up, especially for me. Give me the faith to continue believing that my season is coming. Remove feelings of anger and frustration when things do not seem to be going my way. Reset my focus on doing the work and focusing on You.

Amen

36

For still the vision awaits its appointed time;
it hastens to the end—it will not lie.
If it seems slow, wait for it;
it will surely come; it will not delay.
Habakkuk 2:3 ESV

Put it in writing, because it is not yet time for it to come
true. But the time is coming quickly, and what I show you
will come true. It may seem slow in coming, but wait for it;
it will certainly take place, and it will not be delayed.
Habakkuk 2:3 GNT

Dear God - I thank you for the faith and patience to wait on your vision for my life to come into fruition. I find myself getting antsy about the dreams you placed inside of me. I get tired of waiting and start to question whether they are really in your will. I praise you for reminding me that the vision will come to pass at its appointed time.

No matter how slow it seems, I will wait because I am confident that it will come. I thank you that there is no delay in your timing.

Amen

37

Let all things be done decently and in order.
1 Corinthians 14:40

Father - You have called us to do all things decent and in order. Therefore, I ask that you motivate me to be organized in my work dealings and at home. Give me the unction to be prepared and provide me with a plan for approaching everything that I touch. I understand that my life is meant to be a reflection of you.

Help me to be a good representation, even as it relates to organization. I want to do things in an orderly fashion.

Amen

38

*Show yourself in all respects to be a model of good works,
and in your teaching show integrity, dignity, and sound
speech that cannot be condemned, so that an opponent
may be put to shame, having nothing evil to say about us.*
Titus 2:7-8 ESV

Lord Jesus - I want my reputation to be a positive reflection of the kingdom of heaven. Help me to be an example of you in all that I do. I commit myself to being a model of good works. Let my legacy be on integrity, dignity, and sound speech. Remove character flaws within me that are not like you.

I want to live in a way that does not bring shame to myself or to you. My goal is always to exemplify the life of Christ daily.

Help me to bear witness to who you are, and do not let me contribute to negative comments about who I am by being careless in my actions.

Amen

39

Jesus Christ is the same yesterday and today and forever.
Hebrews 13:8 ESV

Merciful Savior - Thank you for being the ultimate example of consistency. The very makeup of who you are has remained the same from the beginning of time.

I know that my progress hinges on my consistency. Help me to work toward continual development. Let me be consistent in my personal, professional, and spiritual growth. I do not want to be stagnant. Instead, I ask that you make me more like you, even as it relates to my consistency. Show me strategies and techniques for developing healthy habits that become an integral part of who I am.

I know you've called me to be successful in my endeavors. Be with me as I do my part to accomplish my goals by being consistent.

Amen

40

*When Moses' hands grew tired, they took a stone and put
it under him and he sat on it. Aaron and Hur held his
hands up—one on one side, one on the other—so that his
hands remained steady till sunset. So Joshua overcame the
Amalekite army with the sword.*
Exodus 17:12-13 NIV

Lord - I thank you for divine connections. Place those
around me who will lift me up when I grow tired. Like
Moses, I will encounter battles that I cannot win by myself.

I recognize that my team impacts my victories. Bless me
with the type of friends that will hold my hands up so that
they remain steady during times of war. Put people around
me who are specifically designed to help me overcome the
struggles I face on this journey of life.

Help me to be the type of teammate who does the same
for those placed in my path. Make me an Aaron or Hur for
the Moses' who need me to stand steadfast. Teach me how
to lift up my friends in prayer. Show me how to be an asset
in times of need.

Amen

41

But he said to me, "My grace is sufficient for you, for my power is made perfect in weakness." Therefore I will boast all the more gladly about my weaknesses, so that Christ's power may rest on me. That is why, for Christ's sake, I delight in weaknesses, in insults, in hardships, in persecutions, in difficulties. For when I am weak, then I am strong.
2 Corinthians 12:9-10 NIV

Father - I humbly thank you for your grace. I am blessed to know that your power is perfected during my times of weakness. Because of this irrefutable fact, I understand that my weaknesses are not a hindrance.

Even when I cannot get it right on my own, I will come out victorious because of he that is within me.

I will no longer be ashamed of the difficulties I face because I know that when I am weak, then I am strong in you. I will brag about your goodness and exclaim the victory at all times. Regardless of the battle, your word makes it clear that in the end, I win.

Amen

42

For the righteous falls seven times and rises again, but the
wicked stumble in times of calamity.
Proverbs 24:16 ESV

Lord - Give me the resilience to keep getting back up. Sometimes, my failures seem like an indication to quit; but I now know I can rise after every failure because of who I am through Christ.

No matter how big or small, my failures are not the end. My slips and falls are nothing more than testimonies of your greatness. I declare that I will rise again and live to tell the story. I decree victory over every battle that knocks me down.

I praise you for raising me up over and over again because of your love for me. I thank you that when I stumble during times of calamity, I will get back up again.

Amen

43

And Moses built an altar, and
called the name Jehovahnissi.
Exodus 17:15 KJV

Moses built an altar and called it
The Lord is my Banner.
Exodus 17:15 NIV

Jehovah Nissi - Today, I declare that you are my Banner. I will proudly proclaim your glory. I recognize you as the hero of my story, the sole reason for every victory in my life. Let my praise and worship be on display for others to see.

You, father, are the predominate label that composes my being - the image that identifies who I am. Let your light in me be a navigating force that brings others to You. Show through in an undeniable way. I want to be bold and loud about who you are to me.

I celebrate your faithfulness. Use me as a gravitational pull that leads your people closer to you.

Amen.

44

*God saw everything that He had made, and behold, it was
very good and He validated it completely.*
Genesis 1:31 AMP

*A*wesome Father - I thank you that your word is a
reminder of who I am to you. From the beginning
of time, you knew me. You breathed life into my body and
orchestrated a divine plan for me before my parents ever
conceived me.

Sometimes it is so easy to criticize myself. In the stillness
of the night, my mind wanders to my faults, shortcomings,
and imperfections. Right now, I am reminded that you
see me where I am. Regardless of the negative thoughts
roaming in my mind, you made me. You call me good, and
through you I am validated completely.

Help me to recall the beauty that you see in me when I
cannot see it in myself.

Amen

45

*And God said, "Let there be light," and there was light.
God saw that the light was good, and He separated the
light from the darkness."*
Genesis 1:3-4 NIV

Lord - Right now, I come to you asking that you would make me light. Separate me from the darkness of this world and guide me on my mission to be the good I want to see. Help me to illuminate dark situations. Use me as a positive force. Let me shine bright for you in a way that draws all men unto you.

My utmost priority is leading by the life I live. I submit to being your Northern star, a guiding light for those who need to find their way. Convict my spirit when I am tempted to dim my light by committing actions that are not pleasing to you.

Use me as a bright spot that brings joy and hope to those who encounter my spirit.

Amen

46

So God created man in His own image, in the image and likeness of God He created him; male and female He created them.
Genesis 1:27 AMP

*D*ear Creator - Thank you for making me in your image. Because I am made in the likeness of God, I am privileged to walk in special authority.

Through the act of breathing in me, you delegated your power to me. I thank you for calling me to dominate at life. I stand upright in the miraculous beauty of your majesty, and I operate from a place of boldness in you.

I praise you for making clear who I am and whose I am.

Amen

47

*She sets about her work vigorously; her arms are strong for
her tasks.*
Proverbs 31:17

Awesome God – Thank you for the ability to do the work both personally and professionally. Thank you for expanding my creative ideas while also allowing me to carve out time with family.

I acknowledge that it is by your power that I continue to succeed at all that I put my hand to doing. You have truly proven that with you, nothing is impossible. Help me to continue to press toward my dreams. Use me as an example that we don't have to settle or choose. I know that you have called us to rule and reign as mothers, wives, entrepreneurs, and career women. Let it be so in our lives. Guide us on our journey, granting us wisdom every step of the way.

Bless us that we may be a blessing to those around us and that we may show forth your glory in all that we are – in all that we are becoming.

Amen

48

*But you are a chosen people, a royal priesthood, a holy
nation, God's special possession, that you may declare
the praises of him who called you out of darkness into his
wonderful light.*
1 Peter 2:9

Lord - I honor you for your splendid abilities and
amazing grace. Even when I try, my mind cannot fully
comprehend all that you are to me. Your greatness is
indescribable, and your display of love is incredible. None
of my earthly accomplishments make me worthy, and yet
your blessings abound in my life. You desire better for me
than I even want for myself. You allow me to find you by
simply seeking you out.

No matter how I run you away, you consider me chosen.
When I feel inferior, you call me royalty. At moments when
my mind calls me less than, you still consider me your
special possession. Regardless of my faults, you still call me
out of darkness into your marvelous light.

Today, oh God, I am here simply to say Thank you. You
are Alpha and Omega; your wisdom and knowledge are
endless. Your love is mind blowing; I will worship and
praise you forever.

Amen

49

For God hath not given us the spirit of fear; but of power,
and of love, and of a sound mind.
2 Timothy 1:7

Lord - At times, doubt causes me to question my calling. My mind wanders to fears that others may misjudge me or lack faith in my ability to accomplish the outlandish dreams you've placed in my heart. Help me not to shy away from goals because they seem unrealistic. Remind me that you specialize in making the impossible possible for your people.

Make me comfortable with taking up space. Negate any thoughts that would lead me to shrink myself. Let me always recall that fear is not of you but that you have given me power, love, and a sound mind - the three ingredients that authorize me to do anything I set my mind to doing.

Amen

50

*The plans of the diligent lead surely to abundance, but
everyone who is hasty comes only to poverty. Proverbs 21:5*

Father - help me to be diligent in my plan for success.
When I get weary, remind me that true abundance will
always be the result of hard work.

Sometimes, it is easy to consider the easy route, but I
understand that there is no "get rich quick scheme" that
truly pays off. Your word makes clear that haste without a
plan leads to poverty. I want to walk in overflow. For this
reason, I commit to doing the work.

I know that, regardless of the time it takes, you will
honor my sweat equity with measurable results. I thank
you in advance, and I count it done.

Amen

51

*Be not deceived; God is not mocked: for whatsoever a man
soweth, that shall he also reap.*
Galatians 6:7

Gracious God - Your word makes clear that I will always harvest what I plant. I want to make it my mission to plant the type of seeds that grow into positive outcomes. Be with me as I make daily decisions. Remind me that I get out what I put in as it relates to every aspect of my life.

If I want to grow a business, I must put in the grunt work. If I want sound friendships, I must show myself friendly. Nothing I desire will come to me unless I do my part to sow into those desires. Knowing this fact, I ask that you help me as I put my hands to the plow.

Touch my mind and give me the perseverance to do the labor associated with planting a harvest. Show me how to weed out the things that are not pleasing to you. Make me conscious of my actions that I may sow the good that I hope to reap.

Amen

52

Therefore I tell you, do not worry about your life, what you
will eat or drink, or about your body, what you will wear.
Is not life more than food, and the body more than clothes?
Matthew 6:25 KJV

Lord - I sometimes find myself getting anxious about my life and the goals I hope to achieve. I admit that I daydream about certain luxuries and find myself frustrated about how I can obtain more earthly things.

Today, I am reminded that life is about more than a luxurious lifestyle. It is about the ability to be present with those I love, the opportunity to make an impact, and the honor of living an upright life for you. I know that your plan is to prosper me, but help me not to get so engulfed with the idea of prosperity that I lose sight of the things that matter most.

I bind up anxiety about my future and release peace about my present situation. I thank you that you know all and control all. I give the load of it all to you, understanding that you always have my best interest in mind.

Amen

53

Blessed are those who keep his statutes and seek him with all their heart.
Psalms 119:2

Dear God - Guide me and keep me. Let my thoughts be centered on keeping your statutes, and my heart focused on knowing you in a better way.

Sometimes the outside noise of this world distracts me from emphasizing the precepts that matter most. I want to rededicate my energy to finding quiet bouts of time that center me and allow me to seek your will.

Show me more of you in all that I do. Let even the whisper of the wind that gently sways the foliage around me be a revelation of your power. I know that your glory is recognizable in all things.

As I look for you, show me your presence, your grace, your plan in all that my eyes see. Then I will be blessed in ways that are not even comprehendible to me now.

Amen

54

This is my commandment that you love and unselfishly
seek the best for one another, just as I have loved you. No
one has greater love [nor stronger commitment] than to lay
down his own life for his friends.
John 15:13 AMP

Lover of my soul - Help me to keep your commandment by loving unselfishly and seeking the best for those in my life. Don't let me get so caught up in my ambitions that I lose sight of being the friend you have called me to be.

Strengthen my commitment to my team. Be with me as I work to operate from a place of agape love. Show me how to be there when I am needed. Let me be willing to go the extra mile.

Keep me from making everything about myself. I want to be selfless in my role as a friend, loving in a way that mirrors your love for me.

Amen

55

*No discipline seems pleasant at the time, but painful. Later
on, however, it produces a harvest of righteousness and
peace for those who have been trained by it.*
Hebrews 12:11 NIV

Lord - Equip me with the discipline I need to be successful in my endeavors. Help me to embrace the correlation between the sacrifice and the reward. I want to lean into the pain of the process by being focused on the outcomes.

I understand that training my mind, body, and spirit to be disciplined produces a harvest of righteousness and peace. Because I yearn to experience the harvest, I will consistently do the work. Adjust my attitude and reprogram my mindset. Make discipline an integral part of my being.

Give me the grit to repeat hard actions over and over again so that I may reap the benefits in the future.

Amen

56

Here I am! I stand at the door and knock. If anyone hears
my voice and opens the door, I will come in and eat with
that person, and they with me.
Revelation 3:20 NIV

*D*ear God - Thank you for pursuing me. Your love is always openly inviting me to commune with you.

Let me not seek mere earthly guidance, forgetting the value of consultation with you. Help me always to hear your voice and respond by letting you in. I know that your guidance supersedes any other advice or counsel I can receive.

I commit to retaining you in each of my actions. I praise you for the honor and privilege to freely meet with you all the days of my life. I commit to opening the door to my heart that I may be closer to you in all that I do.

Amen

57

Do not let your hearts be troubled. You believe in God;
believe also in me.
John 14:1 NIV

Gracious Savior - Help me not to be afraid when the troubles of life seek to rock my world. Remind me to believe in you confidently and trust you regarding all things.

I thank you for strengthening my faith. Let me hold on to your promises when situations look dim. I want to totally rely on you and not my own inclinations. Be with me as I press forward despite opposition. Show forth your power when it seems impossible for me to win. Remind me to rest in you when I feel tossed about in my thoughts.

I love you, and I trust you with it all.

Amen

58

You will keep in perfect peace those whose minds are
steadfast, because they trust in you.
Isaiah 26:3 NIV

Lord - Regardless of what happens, I vow to trust in you. By following through with this promise, I know that you will keep me in perfect peace. I thank you for continually dwelling in my thoughts. No matter the situation, keep my focus on you.

I want my life to be proof of what happens when you are first. Use me as a light and a testimony of your greatness. Even through bleak times, keep my mind in a state of peace. Protect me from thoughts that weigh me down.

Lift me up like only you can. I thank you in advance.

Amen

59

*The Lord is close to the brokenhearted and saves those who
are crushed in spirit.*
Psalms 34:18 NIV

Dear God - Today, I thank you for who you are. In alignment with your gracious spirit, you choose to be closer to me when I am heartbroken. When I am crushed, you choose to save me, making a beautiful mosaic from what looks like scraps to others. Because you are with me through the disappointments of life, I can press forward.

Help me to feel you when I am at my lowest. Wrap me in your peace and kiss the hurt away. Reveal the purpose for the pain I've endured and show me how to use it for my good. Let everything that was intended to break me make me stronger. Make me over.

Help me come out of tough situations brand new.

Amen

60

Just as the Son of Man did not come to be served, but to serve, and to give his life as a ransom for me. Matthew 20:28 NIV

Lord - Give me a servant mentality. Let the life I live be one of giving to others. Help me to remember your ultimate example when I am tempted to give less than. Remind me that even my career and entrepreneurial endeavors should be designed to meet a need and to solve a problem that helps someone.

Through my success, keep me focused on giving. I never want to get so busy or so high up that I become consumed with my own selfish desires. You displayed to perfection what it means to be a servant leader. Let me be more like you each day, serving every step of the way.

Amen

61

Your word is a lamp for my feet, a light on my path.
Psalms 119:105 NIV

Awesome God - I thank you for your word. As I seek to make the best decisions regarding my ultimate life plan, I ask that you would let your word be a lamp unto my feet.

Light the way as I pursue the path that you designed specifically for me. I want to be open and available to hear what you have to say about my direction.

Today, I pray that I will always seek to know your word and to hear your voice. I realize that I need you, and I cannot make it without you. Order my steps in your word. Show me your way and give me the wherewithal to abide by your principles that I may be all that you have called me to be.

Amen

62

*A cheerful heart is good medicine, but a crushed
spirit dries up the bones.*
Proverbs 17:22 NIV

Lord - We need a dose of joy like never before. Bless us with reasons to smile when the world tells us we should cry. Provide us with moments that heal our souls with laughter instead of fear for tomorrow. Let us find refuge in the positivity left in this world. Give us the strength to uplift each other even when we feel downtrodden and drained of hope.

We acknowledge that you are a healer and a fixer. When life seems unbearably bleak, you make all things new. You are the voice of the voiceless, a very present help in time of need.

Right now, this world needs you like never before. Use me and those around me as your instruments for change. Display your power in our ability to rise when we are justified in sinking. Put a song of joy in our hearts that changes the atmosphere around us. Let us be light amongst the darkness, hope for the hopeless. Let us be the change we want to see.

Overwhelm the indifference with empathy that compels them to act on behalf of those who need their help. Show them that the problems of their sisters and brothers are also their problems - problems impeding upon all of humanity. Convict their spirits and move them to do more.

I know that you are STILL in the midst, and I thank you for challenging me to use the weapon of prayer over despair. Turn it around like only you can. Bless us with cheerful hearts that we may heal our crushed spirits. Help us all to be on the right side of history. Give us the strength to start by sharing a smile.

Amen

63

For with God, nothing shall be impossible.
Luke 1: 37 KJV

Benevolent Father – I thank you that when I call on you, nothing is impossible and that my radical faith emboldens you to do miraculous things in my life. I believe that when I ask you for unheard of things in total belief in your ability, you make it happen.

Right now, I ask that you allow me to walk in the knowledge that you have my best interest in mind. Give me the courage to chase my wildest dreams. I believe you hear me and that you will answer me.

I praise you in advance and count it as done.

Amen

64

*Create in me a clean heart, O God; and renew a right
spirit within me.
Psalms 51:10-19*

Awesome God – I thank you just for being who you are. Create a clean heart in me, O God, and cleanse me of everything that is displeasing to you. Forgive me of my sins as I show grace to those who have hurt me. Help me to live for today and to walk in your will. I understand that I am but a vapor, and you are ultimately in control.

I trust you with tomorrow. I rest in your plan for my life.

I praise you for your kindness, and I thank you for your amazing grace.

Amen

65

He that is without sin among you, let him first
cast a stone at her.
John 8:7 KJV

Loving God – Thank you for your unconditional love for me. I ask that you help me to be more like you. Help me to love unconditionally. Remove my desire to keep score of others' sins or revel in the misfortune of those who have mistreated me.

Take away suspicions and assumptions that make me judge others.

Help me to reflect you. Let my light and my life draw others to you. Thank you for setting me free.

Amen

66

The LORD directs the steps of the godly. He delights in
every detail of their lives.
Psalms 37:23 NLT

Lord – Thank you for your many blessings. I thank you for all that you are and all that you do.

Forgive me for all things that are not like you and make me over again. I praise you that I have a new name. I ask that you guide me, guide my goals, and show me how to align with your will.

Help me to be disciplined and consistent as I work to achieve my goals. Thank you for placing the right resources in place to help me accomplish kingdom purpose. I live to make you proud!

Amen

67

Stand fast therefore in the liberty wherewith Christ hath made us free and be not entangled again with the yoke of bondage.
Galatians 5:1 KJV

Awesome Father – I thank you that my name is free. Thank you for making the ultimate sacrifice that I might walk in the freedom you gifted me from Calvary.

Right now, I bind up anything that would seek to hold me captive. I cast away thoughts and opinions that weigh heavily on my spirit, and I claim total freedom in you.

Thank you for calling me into your marvelous light.

Amen

68

I will instruct you and teach you in the way you should go,
I will counsel you with my loving eye on you.
Psalm 32:8 ESV

Without counsel, plans fail, but with many
advisors they succeed.
Proverbs 15:22 ESV

Lord – Teach me which goals to focus on, and surround me with resources who can advise me on how to succeed at the things I put my hand to doing. Align my desires with yours and help me to be successful in my plans.

I fully trust you, Lord.

Amen

69

And pray in the Spirit on all occasions with all kinds of
prayers and requests. With this in mind, be alert and
always keep on praying for all the Lord's people.
Ephesians 6:18 NIV

God – grant me the vision to form the proper prayer strategy. Teach me how to fight the right way. Bless me to be the best version of myself. Help me to be slow to anger and quick to hear.

Convict my spirit so that I pray continuously. Show me how to love others the way you have caused me to love them. Take away the things in me that are not like you. Make me new, Lord. I trust you to do what only you can do.

Amen

70

Whatever you do, work at it with all your heart, as working
for the Lord, not for human masters.
Colossians 3:23 NIV

Dear Lord – I thank you for my goals. I ask that you help each of my dreams glorify you so that others hear of your wonders and your magnificent love. Let each of my dreams give reverence to you.

Help me to do all things unto you.

Give me the self-discipline to see my dreams to fruition. Keep me focused on the right things.

Amen

71

I press toward the mark for the prize of the high calling of
God in Christ Jesus.
Philippians 3:14

Dear Lord – I thank you for reminding me that you are the ultimate goal. I praise you for the opportunity to delight myself in you. Because of this, I know you will give me the desires of my heart.

I am committed to your ways, and I trust you to do more than I can even imagine.

As I strengthen my connection with you, I ask that you help me produce fruit that blesses your kingdom.

Bless me to experience career growth and give me favor with decision-makers. But more than anything, help me to experience growth in you.

Amen

72

Jabez cried out to the God of Israel, "Oh, that you would bless me and enlarge my territory! Let your hand be with me and keep me from harm so that I will be free from pain." And God granted his request.
1 Chronicles 4:10

All-Knowing Father – I thank you for reminding me of your promises when I begin to feel discouraged.

I trust your plan for my life, and I trust that you will always order my steps. Your word says that you will grant me the desires of my heart. Right now, I trust you with my career endeavors. I believe you for promotions and financial increase.

I thank you for placing me in positions that allow me to add value and grow me as a person. Give me favor as I seek out these positions. Expand my territory and put me on the minds of the right people. I promise that I will glorify you through every win in my life.

Amen

73

*And he who was seated on the throne said, "Behold, I am
making all things new." Also, he said, "Write this down, for
these words are trustworthy and true."*
Revelations 21:5

*D*ear God – I know that you are the ultimate healer.
I thank you for healing the broken places in my life
and in the lives of others. I praise you in advance for taking
away the pain of heartache and disappointment. I rejoice
in the restoration of physical ailments that seek to hold me
back. I know that you can do all things.

Show forth your unmatched power. Make us like new.
I bind up sickness and pain, and I release healing. Shine
down on us and have your way.

Amen

74

*But the fruit of the Spirit is love, joy, peace, patience,
kindness, goodness, faithfulness, gentleness, and self-control.*
Galatians 5:22-23 ESV

Thank you, O perfect God, for your everlasting grace and mercy. I praise you for continuously loving me despite my shortcomings and apparent unworthiness.

You love me even when I am hard to love, and you forgive me when others would have turned their backs on me. I thank you for blessing me with continuous opportunities to be better through you.

Help me to constantly bear the fruit of the spirit. Let me be a true reflection of your unconditional love. Give me contagious joy that spreads like wildfire. Let peace ooze from within me as worry dissipates. Show me how to be patient on this journey, realizing that all things happen in your timing. Let me be good, faithful, and gentle like you. Teach me self-control that helps me take care of temper - slow to anger, willing to listen, and open to growth.

Amen

75

*Know therefore that the Lord your God is God, the faithful
God who keeps covenant and steadfast love with those
who love him and keep his commandments, to a thousand
generations,*
Deuteronomy 7:9 ESV

Lord, you are faithful, and I depend on you. I thank you in advance that as I seek to accomplish my ambitions, you will give me the desires of my heart. Make me a testimony. Use my situation for your glory. While I wait on you, create peace and contentment in my heart. Help me to maintain gratitude while being the best at my current role. Help me to remain focused and willing to give my all.

Amen

76

In the same way, let your light shine before others, that they may see your good deeds and glorify your Father in heaven.
Matthew 5:16 NIV

Beloved Father – I thank you for being the master and ruler of all things.

Your love is boundless, and your heart for people is indescribable. Help me to be more like you. Erase the things in my life that are not pleasing to you and make me over again.

Forgive me for my sins and create in me a clean heart. Help me to live by your principles that I may lead others to you. Let my light shine before men in such a way that my good deeds and moral excellence lead them to glorify you.

Use me for your will and purpose. I want to make you proud.

Amen

77

Be anxious for nothing, but in everything by prayer and supplication, with thanksgiving, let your requests be made known to God; and the peace of God, which surpasses all understanding, will guard your hearts and minds through Christ Jesus.
Philippians 4:6-7

Lord – Please take away every overwhelming spirit that seeks to make me anxious. Remind me of your promises that I may rest in your perfect peace as I navigate through life.

Use me as an example of what happens when we choose to trust you.

Today, I make the decision to lean and depend on you. I know that your plans are to prosper me. I trust that as I do my part, you will guide me in the right direction. Have your way.

Amen

78

Therefore encourage one another and build each other up,
just as in fact you are doing.
1 Thessalonians 5:11

*D*ear God – Today, I ask that you bless my friends and family like never before. You intimately know every issue, need, and desire. I trust that even when I am not aware of the full story, you know all things. Be with them through the ups and downs of life. Bring them closer to you and heal them where needed. Prosper them and keep them in the midst of it all. Help me to maintain the sensitivity to be cognizant of their needs. Let me be willing to lend a hand, be a listening ear, and a shoulder to lean on.

Amen

79

Trust in the Lord with all your heart,
and do not lean on your own understanding.
In all your ways acknowledge him,
and he will make straight your paths.
Proverbs 3:5-6 ESV

Lord – Guard my heart and my mind. Give me peace and help me not to worry even when I feel stuck, frustrated, or uncertain about the future. Help my mind to remain stayed on you. I know that you have the final say.

I trust that you hear my petitions and prayers. When I am tempted to lean on my own understanding, I will rely on you. Chart my course, God. I want to follow your plan. Thank you in advance for granting my requests.

Amen

80

What, then, shall we say in response to these things? If God is for us, who can be against us?
Romans 8:31 NIV

*D*ear God - I thank you that your love comes with benefits. If you are for me, nothing can be against me. Your power and might supersede any obstacle that comes my way, and your grace keeps me even when I do not deserve to be kept. Your high favor covers my life, my dealings, and my future.

I command peace over my mind, understanding that you have already mapped out a plan that ends with me winning.

Amen

81

As the Father loved Me, I also have loved you; abide in My love. If you keep my commandments, you will abide in My love, just as I have kept My father's commandments and abide in His love.
John 15:9-19 NKJV

Lord – I thank you that nothing can separate me from your love.

Regardless of what happens in life, the way you care for me will remain the same. Help me to remember this fact even when I feel lost or alone. Let it guide my life and lead me to demonstrate unconditional love to those around me.

Teach me to always abide in your love by keeping your commandments.

Amen

82

Have I not commanded you? Be strong and courageous.
Do not be afraid; do not be discouraged, for the LORD
your God will be with you wherever you go.
Joshua 1:9

God – I thank you for being in control of my life. Your word tells me not to worry about anything, so I come instead to lay my dreams and ambitions at your feet. Help me to be strong and courageous rather than afraid and discouraged.

I thank you that your favor opens every door.

Bless me to see advancement in my life in accordance with your will. I thank you that you will act on my behalf to create the right outcome, and I claim that I will not worry while I wait.

Amen

83

And without faith it is impossible to please God because anyone who comes to him must believe that he exists and that he rewards those who earnestly seek him.
Hebrew 11:6

*D*ear Lord – Today, I declare that I walk in great immense faith because I serve a great big God.

I understand that my belief is pleasing to you. I believe that you are a rewarder of those who diligently seek you. Right now, I seek your guidance, wisdom, and protection in my life.

I seek your favor as I strive for my heart's desires, and I believe in your ability to grant me those desires. Release your blessing in my life that I may use them as a testimony of your glory. Remove roadblocks and distractions that take my eyes off of the great work you are doing in my life.

I trust you for unlikely blessing and astounding connections that make my wildest dreams come true.

Amen

84

*And you will seek me and find me, when you search for me
with all your heart.*
Jeremiah 29:13 NKJV

Awesome God – I walk confidently in your promises for my life, remembering that I am a daughter of the King.

Let your light shine in my life from the inside out. Turn me into a reflection of you. Make me a world changer and use me for your purpose. Bless my heart and help me to seek after you daily, that each of my wins may be tied to you.

More than all of my earthly desires, I long to be near you. Let me feel your presence continually with me in all that I do. May I always remember to seek you every step of the way.

Amen

85

*Love the Lord your God with all your heart and with all
your soul and with all your mind and with all your strength.
The second is this: 'Love your neighbor as yourself. There is
no commandment greater than these.*
Mark 12:30-31 NIV

*D*ear Lord – Thank you for your word which lends
way to the truth. Thank you for convicting me when
I am wrong and for creating the desire within me to be a
better person each day.

I ask that you help me not to judge others but to focus
on areas in my own life that I should change.

Make gossip disgusting on my lips, and let the words
that come out of my mouth edify you. Break my bad habits,
flaws, and imperfections that I may be an example of you
to those around me. Let my focus be on the right things.

Amen

86

The faithful love of the Lord never ends. His mercies never cease, Great is his faithfulness; his mercies begin afresh each morning... The Lord is good to those who depend on Him, to those who search for him.
Lamentations 3:22-23;25 NLT

*D*ear Lord – I thank you that your faithful love never ends. I worship you because your mercies never cease.

I know that you are good to those who depend on you and who search for you. I understand that the best decision I can make is to do both of these things.

Guide me in every decision I make for my life. Go with me as I come and go. Protect me from unforeseen danger and give me wisdom in difficult situations.

Bless me that I may be a blessing to others. Remove my love for things of this world that keep my focus from you.

Amen

87

Ask, and it shall be given you; seek, and ye shall find;
knock, and it shall be opened unto you: For every one that
asketh receiveth; and he that seeketh findeth; and to him
that knocketh it shall be opened.
Matthew 7:7-8 KJV

God – I refuse to worry because I know who I belong to. Thank you for working everything out for my good.

I believe in your power to make people who seem against me for me. I bind up anything which would seek to block the blessings you have in store for me, and I release favor, overflow, and increase.

I thank you that when I ask, it will be given to me. I ask that you enlarge my territory, bless my personal brand, and provide me with career growth. Open new doors.

Bless me that I might bless others.

Amen

88

I have said these things to you, that in me you may have peace. In the world you will have tribulation. But take heart; I have overcome the world.
John 16:33 ESV

Gracious Father – Thank you for your new mercies every morning. Help me to refocus on being who you have called me to be. Cover me in your peace, removing worry and confusion from my mind.

When I am frustrated, help me to recall that though I may face tribulation in the world, you have overcome the world just for me.

Reset my thoughts to only focus on the things that are pleasing to you. Let me operate in your love today. Make me more like you. Fill me with kindness and grace. Remind me of all that you are to me when my mind drifts to the wrong things.

Amen

89

Are not five sparrows sold for two pennies? And not one of them is forgotten before God. Why, even the hairs of your head are all numbered. Fear not; you are of more value than many sparrows.
Luke 12:6-7
ESV

*D*ear Lord – I thank you that no matter what it looks like, I am not forgotten.

You see me, and you hear my request.

Renew my strength. Give me the stamina to finish what I start. Provide me with the wisdom to make the right connections and the courage to properly utilize these connections. Equip me with what it takes to be successful and help me to make a difference. I want to stay on course. Be with me as I continue toward the finish line.

Amen

90

O Lord, You are my God; I will exalt You and praise Your
name, for in perfect faithfulness You have done marvelous
things, things planned long ago.
Isaiah 25:1 NIV

God – I thank you for the ability to influence those around me. Help me not to get weary in well-doing. Continue to give me the will power and discipline to make a difference.

Bless me with ideas and collaborations which draw people to my good works, and inspire them to also do good in the world. Use me as your vessel.

Push me in the direction you would have me to go. Forgive me for my sins and make me over again. Thank you for the marvelous things you have done and the marvelous things you will do.

Amen

91

Love the Lord your God with all your heart and with all
your soul and with all your mind and with all your strength.
The second is this: 'Love your neighbor as yourself. There is
no commandment greater than these.
Mark 12:30-31 NIV

*D*ear Lord – I thank you for compelling me to abide in love.

Fill me with compassion and empathy for others, that I may be moved to love my neighbor as I love myself. Help me to be more selfless in my desires.

Use me to make a mark that matters. Give me a heart for humanity and remind me to act as a representative of your love.

My greatest desire is to please you. I know that loving your people is pleasing to you, so I vow to operate from a place of love in all that I do.

Amen

92

His divine power has given us everything we need for life
and godliness through our knowledge of him who called us
by His own glory and goodness.
2 Peter 1:3 NIV

*A*mazing Savior – I thank you for that I am blessed with everything I need in this life through your divine power.

When the cares of this world rock me, let my knowledge of you be a steadfast anchor. You love me enough to equip me with what I need to manage the surges, slips, highs, and lows. Through it all, I am confident that you will never leave me or forsake me.

Amen

93

She is clothed with strength and dignity, and she laughs without fear of the future. Proverbs 31:25 NIV

Magnificent Creator - Today, I walk in authority to be every bit of who you've called me to be. I thank you for the freedom to maneuver through this journey of life without the bondage of societal or familial restrictions.

I release any baggage that places constraints on my . I laugh without fear of the future because of the You in me. I thank you that I am fearfully and wonderfully made. Despite hiccups, mistakes, and shortcomings you love me still

As 1 of 1, I assume pride and conviction in who I am. Help me to demonstrate the love of Christ not only to those around me but also to myself. When I question it all, I thank you for reminding me that I am worthy.

Amen.

94

But Jesus looked at them and said, "With man this is impossible, but with God all things are possible.
Matthew 19:26 ESV

Dear God - I know that your plans for my life are so magnificent that I can barely comprehend them.

Keep me focused on my ambitions. Help me avoid being the enemy of my own success by putting a cap on what I believe I can accomplish.

When doubt sneaks in, remind me that I can do anything. Flood me with the confidence to leap. I want to fulfill every God-given desire you have placed within me. I thank you in advance for your endless power. Blow my mind, Lord. I am ready.

Amen.

95

*It is in vain that you rise up early and go late to rest, eating
the bread of anxious toil; for he gives to his beloved sleep.*
Psalm 127:2 ESV

Gracious God - Give me the strength to Choose peace over perfection. Help me to find contentment in doing my best and forgetting the rest.

Although you have called us to work as unto you and not unto man, you have also called us to live in peace that surpasses our own understanding. Teach me how to balance these concepts as I strive to accomplish my dreams. Grant me clarify and wisdom on systems and processed that are best suited for my life.

Help me to be okay with asking for assistance when I need it the most.

Calm my thoughts and emotions when I feel anxious and bring me back tto the still waters of your love. I thank you that my best is always good enough. Free me from the crippling effects of perfectionism, and let me bask in your rest. Amen.

96

*"Finally, believers, whatever is true, whatever is honorable
and worthy of respect, whatever is right and confirmed by
God's word, whatever is pure and wholesome, whatever
is lovely and brings peace, whatever is admirable and of
good repute; if there is any excellence, if there is anything
worthy of praise, think continually on these things [center
your mind on them, and implant them in your heart]."*
Philippians 4:8

Dear God - Thank you for reminding me how to center my thoughts.

There is so much visibility to tragedy and bad news that it sometimes becomes overwhelming. Despite what it looks like, help me not to be consumed with negativity and pessimism.

I want to be aware of the world around me while also balancing its effects on my state of being. Bring my thoughts back to the right things. Let my focus be on the good. Help me not to lose sight of everyday blessings. Keep me uplifted by giving me the strength to implant good in my heart. Amen.

97

For I know the plans I have for you," declares the Lord,
"plans to prosper you and not to harm you, plans to give
you hope and a future.
Jeremiah 29:11 NIV

Awesome God - I thank you that your divine plan for my life supersedes my own desires.

I know that, even when things do not go according to my own will, your will is bigger and better. I believe that you orchestrated every twist and turn in my life before I was even conceived, and that you are crafting a story that ultimately lands me right where I need to be.

Today, I submit my will to yours. I trust that every single thing at play in my life is working together for my good. I acknowledge your power, might, and ability to foresee the right outcome. No matter what it looks like in the natural, I know that I win in the end.

Amen

98

I praise you because I am fearfully and wonderfully made;
your works are wonderful; I know that full well.
Psalm 139:14 NIV

Awesome God - Today, I thank you that I am emboldened to take up space and consume rooms.

I recognize that You did not design me to be invisible.

Your plan was never for me to fit into a box or cower at the thought of being different. I am empowered through you to be a warrior for those things which are right. Carry me upward as I operate in your will for my life.

Here I am. I surrender myself to be used as your vessel for greatness. Help me lift others, inspiring them to see themselves as You see us.

Amen

99

Behold, I am doing a new thing;
now it springs forth, do you not perceive it?
I will make a way in the wilderness
and rivers in the desert.
Isaiah 43:19

*D*ear God - I thank you for the joy, restoration, and love of family.

I cannot always fix everything, but today I am reminded that when I send my concerns up to you, they are always in the best hands. You make all things new, and I worship you for it.

Amen.

100

*And you will seek me and find me when you s
earch for me with all your heart.*
Jeremiah 29:13 NKJV

*D*earest Savior – I thank you for making yourself
assessable to me.

Although I am unworthy, you still allow me to seek and
find you. Make my heart's greatest desire the need to know
you more.

Craft my dreams and vision around a greater relationship
with you.

As I seek you, let my desire to know you better transfer
to all I encounter.

Amen

Acknowledgements

"If you want to go fast, go alone. If you want to go far, go together." – African Proverb

All of who I am results from the countless prayers and support of friends and family who dedicate themselves to forever lifting me up. There is no way that I can begin to list each person who has impacted my ability to author this book, but I would be remiss if I did not try.

Gran, Granny, and Paw-Paw, thank you for being living examples of Christ. Your commitment to God paved the way for a legacy of believers who are kept by your prayers daily.

Mama, I thank you for always believing that I can do anything. There is no doubt or judgment in your love. It is truly unconditional, healing me every step of the way. You make up for everything that I thought I lacked. You got it right with us, no matter how much you question it. I look at myself and see you in my style, my grace, my determination, and my ability to see the best in others. I could never repay you for all the good you planted within me, but I hope you are proud of the way I have grown.

To my sisters, Kim, Kendra, and Kyla, I have always felt commissioned with the duty to be the best influence a big sister could be. Because of you three, I give my all. I love you and wish you well in accomplishing all your dreams. I hope you understand that success is not about money and titles so much as it is about love, peace, and happiness. Do not let this world convince you otherwise.

Dearest Kyrie, your very existence is the result of prayers cried out to God. Your birth baptized me with a new level of spirituality and motivates me to be better. I hope you know that I go harder because of you. Thank you for restoring my faith and teaching me newfound strength.

To my husband, Bakari, we started our journey with morning prayers and a whole lot of faith. Look how far we have come since then. Thank you for evolving into a better partner each day. Where I am weak you make me strong. The power of God in our lives is so evident in my written prayers that I felt compelled to bless others by sharing them. I hope you always know what your love means to me.

Dad, so much of my ambition is tied to you. Your support fuels me and keeps me focused on the big picture. You are ever present in my humor, mannerisms, inflections, drive, and even in Ky's smirk. God sprinkled the best of you throughout us – a blessing I will never regret.

To Zuri Vaughn, Kendra Ceasar, and Adecia Lewis, thank you for empowering me to dream out loud. Sometimes, you all believe in me more than I believe in myself. When I am nervous about the next big leap you embolden me to close my eyes and jump. You all are the best Goal Friends any girl could have in this life.

Naomi Walker, Brittany Causey, Bethany Blackson, Natalie Grigsby, Andrell Cooper, and Skyla Banks, there is never a time you are not willing to go the extra mile. Thank you for being crisis management and a very present help in time of need.

Made in the USA
Coppell, TX
20 December 2020

46191272R00066